When I Am Gloomy
በሚደብረኝ ጊዜ

Sam Sagolski
Illustrated by Daria Smyslova

www.kidkiddos.com
Copyright ©2025 by KidKiddos Books Ltd.
support@kidkiddos.com

All rights reserved. No part of this book may be reproduced in any form or by any electronic or mechanical means, including information storage and retrieval systems, without written permission from the publisher, except in the case of a reviewer, who may quote brief passages embodied in critical articles or in a review.
First edition, 2025

Translated from English by Sosna Assefa
ከእንግሊዝኛ የተተረጎመው በሶስና አሰፋ

Library and Archives Canada Cataloguing in Publication
When I Am Gloomy (English Amharic Bilingual edition)/Shelley Admont
ISBN: 978-1-83416-783-1 paperback
ISBN: 978-1-83416-784-8 hardcover
ISBN: 978-1-83416-782-4 eBook

Please note that the English and Amharic versions of the story have been written to be as close as possible. However, in some cases they differ in order to accommodate nuances and fluidity of each language.

One cloudy morning, I woke up feeling gloomy.

በአንድ ደመናማ ጠዋት፣ ስነቃ ደብሮኝ ነበር።

I got out of bed, wrapped myself in my favorite blanket, and walked into the living room.

ከአልጋ ወረድኩ እና በምወደው አልጋ ልብስ ተሸፋፍኜ ወደ ሳሎን ተራመድኩ።

"Mommy!" I called. "I'm in a bad mood."

"እማዬ!" ብዬ ተጣራሁ። "ደብሮኛል።"

Mom looked up from her book. "Bad? Why do you say that, darling?" she asked.

እማዬ ከያዘችው መጽሃፍ ቀና አለች። "ደብሮኛል? ለምን እንደዛ አልሽ የኔ ውድ?" በማለት ጠየቀቺኝ።

"Look at my face!" I said, pointing to my furrowed brows. Mom smiled gently.

"ፊቴን ተመልከቺው!" አልኩኝ የተኮማተሩ ቅንድቦቼ ላይ እያጠቀምኩ። እማዬ ፈገግ አለች።

"I don't have a happy face today," I mumbled. "Do you still love me when I'm gloomy?"

"ዛሬ ፊቴ ደስተኛ አይደለም" በማለት አጉረመረምኩ። "በሚደብረኝ ጊዜ ትወጂኛለሽ?"

"Of course I do," Mom said. "When you're gloomy, I want to be close to you, give you a big hug, and cheer you up."

"አዎ በትክክል" አለች እማዬ። "በሚዲብርሽ ጊዜ ለአንቺ ቅርብ መሆን፣ አንቺን ማቀፍ እና ማነቃቃት እፈልጋለሁ።"

That made me feel a little better, but only for a second, because then I started thinking about all my other moods.

ያ የተሻለ ስሜት እንዲሰማኝ አደረገ፣ ነገር ግን ለትንሽ ጊዜ ብቻ ነበር ምክንያቱም ስለሌሎች ስሜቶቼ ማሰብ ጀመርኩ።

"So… do you still love me when I'm angry?"
"ስለዚህ... በምናዴድ ጊዜም ትወጂኛለሽ?"

Mom smiled again. "Of course I do!"
እማዬ አሁንም ፈገግ አለች። "አዎ በትክክል!"

"Are you sure?" I asked, crossing my arms.
"እርግጠኛ ነሽ?" ብዬ ጠየቅኩ እጄን አጣምሬ።

"Even when you're mad, I'm still your mom. And I love you just the same."

"በምትናደጂ ጊዜም እናትሽ ነኝ። እና በተመሳሳይ ሁኔታ እወድሻለሁ።"

I took a big breath. "What about when I'm shy?" I whispered.

ትልቅ ትንፋሽ ወሰድኩ። "በማፍር ጊዜስ?" አልኩኝ በመንሾካሾክ።

"I love you when you're shy too," she said. "Remember when you hid behind me and didn't want to talk to the new neighbor?"

"በምታፍሪም ጊዜም እወድሻለሁ" አለች። "ከአዲሱ ጎረቤት ጋር ላለማውራት ከኋላዬ የተደበቅሽበት ቀን ትዝ ይልሻል?"

I nodded. I remembered it well.

ራሴን ነቀነኩ። በደንብ አስታውሼዋለሁ።

"And then you said hello and made a new friend. I was so proud of you."

"ከዚያ ሰላም አልሽ እና አዲስ ጓደኛ አፈራሽ። በጣም ኮርቼብሽ ነበር።"

"Do you still love me when I ask too many questions?" I continued.

"በጣም ብዙ ጥያቄዎችን በምጠይቅ ጊዜም ትወጂኛለሽ?" በማለት ቀጠልኩ።

"When you ask a lot of questions, like now, I get to watch you learn new things that make you smarter and stronger every day," Mom answered. "And yes, I still love you."

"ልክ እንደ አሁኑ ብዙ ጥያቄዎችን በምትጠይቂ ጊዜ፣ ጎበዝ እና ጠንካራ የሚያደርጉሽን አዳዲስ ነገሮች ስትማሪ ማየት እችላለሁ" አለች እማዬ። "እና አዎ፣ አሁንም እወድሻለሁ።"

"What if I don't feel like talking at all?" I continued asking.

"ከነጭራሹ ማውራት ካልፈለኩስ?" በማለት ጥያቄዬን ቀጠልኩ።

"Come here," she said. I climbed into her lap and rested my head on her shoulder.

"ነይ እስኪ" አለች። ጭኗ ላይ ተቀመጥኩ እና ጭንቅላቴን ትከሻዋ ላይ አሳረፍኩ።

"When you don't feel like talking and just want to be quiet, you start using your imagination. I love seeing what you create," Mom answered.

"ማውራት በማትፈልጊበት እና ዝም ማለት በምትፈልጊበት ጊዜ፣ ምናብሽን መጠቀም ትጀምሪያለሽ። የምትፈጥሪያቸውን ነገሮች መመልከት እወዳለሁ" አለች እማዬ።

Then she whispered in my ear, "I love you when you're quiet too."

ከዚያ ወደ ጆሮዬ ተጠጋች እና በሹክሹክታ "ዝም ስትዪም እወድሻለሁ።" አለቺኝ።

"But do you still love me when I'm afraid?" I asked.

"ግን በምፈራ ጊዜም ትወጂኛለሽ?" ብዬ ጠየቅኩ።

"Always," said Mom. "When you're scared, I help you check that there are no monsters under the bed or in the closet."

"ሁሌም" አለች እማዬ። "በምትፈሪ ጊዜ፣ አልጋው ስር ወይም ቁም ሳጥን ውስጥ ጭራቅ እንደሌለ ለመፈተሽ አግዝሻለሁ።"

She kissed me on the forehead. "You are so brave, my sweetheart."
ግንባሬን ሳመችኝ፡፡ "በጣም ጀግና ነሽ፣ የኔ ጣፋጭ፡፡"

"And when you're tired," she added softly, "I cover you with your blanket, bring you your teddy bear, and sing you our special song."

"እና ደግሞ በሚዲክምሽ ጊዜ" አለች ለስለስ ብላ፣ "በአልጋ ልብስ እሸፍንሽ እና አሻንጉሊትሽን አምጥቼ ልዩ መዝሙራችንን እዘምርልሻለሁ።"

"What if I have too much energy?" I asked, jumping to my feet.

"ከመጠን በላይ ኃይል ቢኖረኛስ?" ብዬ ጠየቅኩ እየዘለልኩ።

She laughed. "When you're full of energy, we go biking, skip rope, or run around outside together. I love doing all those things with you!"

ሳቀች። "ኃይልሽ ሙሉ ሲሆን፣ ብስክሌት ለመንዳት፣ ገመድ ለመዝለል ወይም ውጪ አብሮ ለመሮጥ እንወጣለን። እነዚያን ነገሮች በሙሉ ከአንቺ ጋር ማድረግ እወዳለሁ!"

"But do you love me when I don't want to eat broccoli?" I stuck out my tongue.

"ብሮኮሊ መብላት በማልፈልግ ጊዜ ግን ትወጂኛለሽ?" አልኩኝ ምላሴን አውጥቼ።

Mom chuckled. "Like that time you slipped your broccoli to Max? He liked it a lot."

እማዬ ሳቅ አለች። "ብሮኮሊሽን ለማክስ እንደሰጠሸው ጊዜ? እሱ ወዶት ነበር።"

"You saw that?" I asked.
"አየተሺኛል?" ብዬ ጠየቅኩ።

"Of course I did. And I still love you, even then."
"አዎ አይቼሻለሁ። እና ግን እንደዚያም ሆኖ እወድሻለሁ።"

I thought for a moment, then asked one last question:

ለአፍታ አሰብኩ እና አንድ የመጨረሻ ጥያቄ ጠየቅኩ፣

"Mommy, if you love me when I'm gloomy or mad… do you still love me when I'm happy?"

"እማዬ፣ በሚደብረኝ ወይም በምናደድ ጊዜ የምትወጂኝ ከሆነ… ደስተኛ ስሆንም ትወጂኛለሽ?"

"Oh, sweetheart," she said, hugging me again, "when you're happy, I'm happy too."

"ኦ የኔ ጣፋጭ" አለች እና በድጋሚ አቅፋኝ "ደስተኛ ስትሆኒ እኔም ደስተኛ ነኝ" አለች።

She kissed me on the forehead and added, "I love you when you're happy just as much as I love you when you're sad, or mad, or shy, or tired."

ግንባሬ ላይ ሳመችኝ እና "ደስተኛ ስትሆኒ ልክ በሚከፋሽ፣ በምትናደጂበት፣ በምታፍሪበት ወይም በሚደክምሽ ጊዜ እንደምወድሽ እወድሻለሁ።" አለቺኝ።

I snuggled close and smiled. "So... you love me all the time?" I asked.

ተጠጋኋት እና ፈገግ አልኩ። "ስለዚህ... ሁልጊዜ ትወጂኛለሽ? ብዬ ጠየቅኩ።

"All the time," she said. "Every mood, every day, I love you always."

"ሁልጊዜ" አለች። "በሁሉም አይነት ስሜት፣ በየዕለቱ፣ ሁሌም እወድሻለሁ።"

As she spoke, I started feeling something warm in my heart.

በምትናገርበት ጊዜ ልቤ ውስጥ ሙቀት ተሰማኝ።

I looked outside and saw the clouds floating away. The sky was turning blue, and the sun came out.

ወደ ውጪ ተመለከትኩ እና ደመናዎቹ ሲንሳፈፉ አየሁ። ሰማዩ ሰማያዊ ሆነ እና ጸሃይ ወጣች።

It looked like it was going to be a beautiful day after all.

ቆንጆ ቀን የሚሆን ይመስላል።

www.ingramcontent.com/pod-product-compliance
Lightning Source LLC
LaVergne TN
LVHW072008060526
838200LV00010B/298